Cats Rule!

Snap books®

Cat CARE

Nutrition, Exercise, Grooming, and More

by Carly J. Bacon

CAPSTONE PRESS
a capstone imprint

The author dedicates this book with love to her niece, Kaija, who has always shown a natural empathy toward all animals.

Snap Books are published by Capstone
1710 Roe Crest Drive, North Mankato, Minnesota 56003
www.mycapstone.com

Library of Congress Cataloging-in-Publication Data
Bacon, Carly J., author.
  Cat care : nutrition, exercise, grooming, and more / by Carly J. Bacon.
    pages cm — (Snap books. Cats rule!)
  Audience: Ages 9-11.
  Audience: K to grade 3.
  Summary: "Describes the responsibilities of cat care, including feeding, grooming, and veterinary care"—Provided by publisher.
  Includes bibliographical references and index.
  ISBN 978-1-4914-8399-2 (library binding)
  ISBN 978-1-4914-8411-1 (eBook PDF)
1. Cats—Juvenile literature. 2. Cats—Equipment and supplies—Juvenile literature.
3. Cats—Food—Juvenile literature. I. Title.
  SF445.7.B327 2016
  636.8'083—dc23   2015032922

Editorial Credits
Carrie Sheely and Alesha Halvorson, editors
Philippa Jenkins, designer
Svetlana Zhurkin, media researcher
Steve Walker, production specialist

Printed and bound in US

We would like to thank Laurie Patton, Regional Director, TICA Southeast, for her invaluable help in the preparation of this book.

Photo Credits
Capstone Press: Philippa Jenkins, back cover and throughout, Karon Dubke, 28, 29; Dreamstime: Oscar Williams, 13; iStockphoto: MikaTrta, 11, RyersonClark, 25 (top); Shutterstock: Alena Ozerova, 5, Andrey_Kuzmin, 26, Drozdowski, 8, Eric Isselee, 14, Evgeny Karandaev, 7, Evgenyi, 6, 25 (bottom), IrinaK, 17 (bottom), Ivonne Wierink, 15, Lubava, 19, Michael Pettigrew, 23, MidoSemsem, 4, Natalya Onishchenko, 16, Okssi, cover, Oleksandr Schevchuk, 18, Sergey Gerashchenko, 24, Svetoslav Radkov, 17 (top), Tarapong Srichaiyos, 21, Volt Collection, 20, Yellowj, 22; Svetlana Zhurkin, 9.

Table of Contents

CHAPTER 1

Cat Companions

If you love cats, you're in good company. More than 30 percent of U.S. households include cats. A cat can become a friend and a beloved member of your family. But it's more than just falling in love with beautiful markings and big eyes. Owning a pet is a big responsibility. It's up to you to help your cat live a long, happy life. Are you up to the challenge?

Did You Know?

Zzzz! Cats sleep an average of 13 to 14 hours each day.

Cats can be excellent household companions.

CHAPTER 2

Time to Eat!

Nutrition is an important part of cat care. While fruits and veggies do human bodies good, they aren't the best for cats. That means no sneaking the brussels sprouts to your cat under the table! Many foods that people eat, such as onions, chocolate, and grapes, can harm your cat.

Cats are meat-eaters, so a high-protein diet is important. But that doesn't mean they should share bites of your cheeseburger. Never give human food to your cat unless your veterinarian advises it. A high-quality cat food has the vitamins and nutrients your cat needs.

Cat food is available in both canned and dry form called kibble. Canned food contains more water than dry food. That helps take care of nutrition and **hydration** in one step. When choosing cat food, ask your veterinarian for advice and read the nutritional labels. Look for food that's high in protein such as beef, lamb, or chicken. The food should contain little or no filler such as wheat, soy, or corn.

hydration—the act of drinking enough water to stay healthy

As your cat ages, its nutritional needs change. Kittens need more fat for healthy development. Adult cats should eat lower-calorie food to avoid becoming overweight. At about age seven, a cat needs food made for senior cats. Foods are also designed for cats with health issues, such as kidney disease or food allergies.

Cats love treats! However, they should be given to cats in moderation.

Greenery and Cats

Green plants are irresistible to many cats. But many common houseplants are poisonous to them, including daffodil bulbs, oleander, and poinsettias. Lilies are especially dangerous. When in doubt about whether a plant is safe, ask your veterinarian. Signs that your cat may have eaten a poisonous plant include breathing difficulty, drooling, vomiting, diarrhea, and extreme thirst. If your cat has these symptoms, call your vet immediately.

Stay Hydrated

Water is just as important for cats as it is for people. Water makes up 80 percent of most cats' bodies. That sounds like a lot, right? A dehydrated cat can have problems with **circulation**, digestion, and removing waste from its body.

Keep fresh water available to your cat at all times. You might want to get a pet drinking fountain, which keeps the water flowing, fresh, and filtered. If you don't have a fountain, change the water daily. If your cat drinks more water than usual or is isn't drinking at all, it may be sick. Check with your vet right away.

Cat Fountains

You can buy a cat drinking fountain from most stores or websites that carry pet supplies. You'll also want to buy a stainless steel bowl for the fountain. Just like people, cats can get pimples. Plastic bowls can be the cause.

circulation—the movement of blood through the body

Your cat's water bowl should be cleaned every day.

Exercise and Diet

Studies show that more than 50 percent of pet cats in the United States are overweight. Just like people, cats become overweight when they eat too much and exercise too little. Overweight cats are more likely to develop health problems such as **diabetes** and **arthritis**.

In the wild, cats eat about seven small meals a day. Some owners mimic this by leaving dry cat food out for their cats to nibble throughout the day. But some cats will eat all the food at once. These cats need to be on a feeding schedule. Cats should be fed at least twice a day. An automated feeder will help you stay on schedule if you can't be home at feeding time.

diabetes—a disease in which there is too much sugar in the blood
arthritis—a disease that makes bone joints swollen and painful

Regular visits to the vet can help determine your cat's best feeding schedule.

Some cat breeds naturally weigh more than others. For example, male Maine Coon cats can weigh up to 18 pounds (8.2 kilograms). On the other hand, male Singapuras average 6 to 7 pounds (2.7 to 3.2 kg). Ask your vet about your cat's ideal weight and how much food you should feed it.

If your cat is overweight, ask your vet how to help it lose weight in a healthy way. If a cat drops weight too fast, it can cause life-threatening liver problems. Cats that stop eating completely can get sick very quickly. Call your vet right away if your cat isn't eating.

Maine Coons (below) reach their full size between the ages of 3 and 5 years old.

Did You Know?

The heaviest domestic cat on record weighed 46.8 pounds (21.2 kilograms)! Himmy lived in Australia and died at age 10.

Checking Kitty's Weight

Feel your cat's ribs and then look down at its body from above. Your cat is at a healthy weight if you can slightly feel the ribs and if it has a slight waist when viewed from above. If your cat's ribs are very easy to feel and it has a pronounced waist, your cat is underweight. An overweight cat's ribs are difficult to feel. It has either no visible waist or its body curves outward at the middle.

CHAPTER 3

Playtime!

The second part of keeping your cat trim and healthy is regular exercise. You may notice that your cat gets bursts of energy during certain times of the day. Pay attention to your cat's habits and make the most of these playful spurts. Playing is important for your cat's health and can be fun for both of you.

Different cats prefer different kinds of play. Notice what your cat responds to best. Also, your cat's likes and dislikes might change as it ages. A senior cat may not have as much energy or motivation to play as a younger cat. You may need to get creative when encouraging an older cat to play.

crepuscular—active during twilight

Get your kitty moving with a game of chase-and-fetch with a small ball.

Did You Know?

Cats are **crepuscular**, which means they are most active at dawn and dusk. Has your cat ever tried to wake you up to play at the crack of dawn?

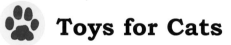

🐾 Toys for Cats

Just like kids, cats need toys. But cat toys don't have to be expensive or high-tech. A paper bag on the floor can entertain a cat for a long time. Remove any handles on the bag, which could choke your cat. Many cats can't resist jumping into a cardboard box. Table tennis balls and empty toilet paper rolls are also items that your cat may enjoy.

When you're home, join in to make playtime more exciting. Tap the back of a paper bag to grab your cat's interest. Or drag a ribbon around the house for your cat to chase. Make sure to supervise though. Ribbon and yarn can be choking hazards. Never let your cat play with plastic bags. Cats can suffocate in these bags.

Toys available at pet supply stores can be fun as well. Make toys move like a cat's natural **prey**. Outdoor cats chase birds, mice, and bugs. A laser pointer mimics a flying bug. Try making a small stuffed animal on a string bounce like a hopping bunny. Make a ribbon slither like a snake in the dirt. Be sure to let your cat "win" these games. A cat may lose interest if it never catches the fake prey.

Your cat may like different colored or textured toys.

prey—an animal hunted by another animal for food

19

CHAPTER 4

Pretty Kitties and Spa Days

For everyday grooming, cats get a gold star. If you've ever had a cat lick your hand, you know how rough its tongue is. Cats' tongues help them remove dirt and dead fur. They also help them spread natural oils, called **sebum**, through their fur. By grooming with its tongue, a cat helps its coat stay shiny, waterproof, and tangle-free. Grooming even helps cats stay cool. When they cover their fur with saliva, their body temperatures drop as the saliva evaporates. Cats can't sweat as much as people do, and they don't usually pant like dogs.

Did You Know?

If a cat does pant, it could be a sign of illness. Vet care may be needed.

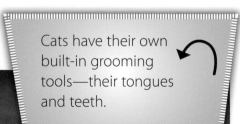

Cats have their own built-in grooming tools—their tongues and teeth.

Although cats do a good job of cleaning themselves, they should be brushed with a pet brush at least once a week. This helps reduce shedding and prevent **hairballs**. If your cat has long hair, you'll need to brush it every day. Hairballs can cause vomiting and constipation. If hairballs become a problem even with regular brushing, consider feeding your cat a food made to prevent hairballs.

Brushing your cat removes dirt, grease, dead hair, and dead skin from its coat.

sebum—an oily liquid produced by the skin glands
hairball—a ball of fur that lodges in a cat's stomach

Homemade Shampoo

Never use shampoo for humans on your cat. Cat shampoo is available at pet supply stores. You can also make your own cat shampoo by mixing these ingredients in a clean bottle:

- 1 cup (237 milliliters) white or apple vinegar
- 1 cup (237 mL) natural liquid dish soap
- 4 cups (946 mL) water

 Bath Time

It's usually not necessary to bathe cats, which is a good thing. Most cats aren't big fans of getting wet! However, cats can sometimes get into messes bigger than their grooming skills can handle. If your cat gets into something that's very dirty or sticky, it may need a bath.

Cat baths are generally a two-person job, so ask an adult to help. You can bathe your cat in a sink or tub. Make sure you use lukewarm water. Have a large, fluffy towel nearby. The first step is to pour the water gently over your cat with a cup or pitcher. Be careful to avoid the cat's eyes, ears, and nose. Once the fur is wet, gently lather with a shampoo made for cats. Then carefully rinse until all the soap is out. You may need to rinse more than once.

If your cat's face is dirty, wipe it gently with a damp washcloth. Don't use shampoo near your cat's face, since it may get into its eyes. To dry, wrap your cat in the towel and gently massage its fur. When done, praise your cat and give it a treat.

After a bath praise your cat with its favorite treat.

🐾 Feline Manis and Pedis

Cats scratch to mark their territories, strengthen muscles, and reduce stress. To prevent damage to curtains and furniture, keep your cat's claws trimmed. Regular claw trimming also reduces accidental scratches during playtime. A cat's claws must be trimmed correctly with a clipper made especially for cats. This can be tricky, and you should always ask an adult for help. Cat trees or scratching posts give your cat appropriate places to use their claws.

Some people choose to declaw their cats' front paws. Declawing is banned in many European countries and some U.S. cities. There are many reasons to not declaw your cat. It can affect a cat's balance and make it less able to survive if it gets lost outdoors. Some vets won't do the procedure because they consider it to be invasive. It involves removing bone so that the claws won't grow back.

Dental Care

If your cat has plaque, receding gums, or is drooling, it may have gum disease or tooth decay. Your vet can clean your cat's teeth, but it can be expensive and unpleasant for your cat. Regular home tooth care is important. Get your cat used to teeth brushing when it is a kitten. You can buy cat toothpaste and toothbrushes at your local pet supply store.

 Bringing Kitty Home

A cat may slip outside and get lost. A tag with the cat's name and your contact information on its collar will help any finder return your cat to you. Some owners have a vet put a microchip in their cats. If a microchipped cat gets lost, a vet or humane society can retrieve your contact information by scanning the microchip.

 Dirty Chores

While most cat owners don't enjoy cleaning litter boxes, it's a necessary chore. If you use scoopable or clumping litter, scoop out the clumps of waste every day. If you use crystal, clay, or any other type of non-clumping litter, you'll need to change the litter about every other day. Try to use the same kind of litter all the time. Your cat may not like different kinds of litter or be upset by the change.

Cats are less likely to relieve themselves around the house if the litter box is clean. Cats are more sensitive to smells than humans. If you can smell the box, just think about how bad it smells to your cat. That's a good reason not to use a covered litter box. Covered litter boxes trap the odor inside. They also may not give your cat much room to move around.

Did You Know?

If your cat suddenly stops using its litter box, it could be a sign of illness such as a urinary tract infection or kidney or liver issues. Call your vet right away.

Check-ups

Annual vet visits are important for your cat. Check-ups and vaccines are necessary to prevent illness and catch any health issues. Vaccines are important to keep your cat from developing fatal diseases such as **feline distemper** and rabies.

All owners should have their cats spayed or neutered. Besides preventing unwanted kittens, spaying or neutering your cat has many other benefits. Unneutered male cats are much more likely to mark their territories by spraying urine in the house. Spaying and neutering also helps protect cats against cancer of the breast and reproductive organs.

feline distemper—a serious and sometimes fatal cat disease that involves fever, vomiting, diarrhea, and dehydration

PROJECT

Cat House and Bed

Treat your cat to its own house and bed. Be sure to use materials without small pieces that could be a choking hazard. Let your creativity run wild! When you've finished, watch your cat investigate the house. Some cats need time to adjust to a new item. Give your cat the space and time it needs to explore.

What You Need:

- cardboard box large enough for your cat to turn around
- utility knife
- 2 pieces of fleece fabric, large enough to fit inside the box.
- ruler
- masking tape
- fabric scissors
- pillow stuffing
- colored markers or scraps of fabric

What You Do:

1. Ask an adult to help you cut a hole in the side of the box with the utility knife. The hole should be large enough for your cat to enter and exit freely.

2. Put the two pieces of fleece fabric together so that the edges line up.

3. Measure 4 inches (10 cm) in from each edge of the fabric and mark with masking tape.

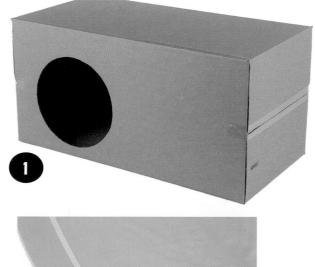

4. With the scissors, cut 1-inch (2.5-cm) strips on the edges of your fabric up to the masking tape. This creates fringe on all four sides.

5. On three of the sides, tie the top strip with the matching bottom strip.

6. Use the open side to stuff the pillow stuffing into the cat bed.

8. Remove masking tape.

7. Tie the strips on your last side together so that the stuffing stays inside

9. Place the bed inside the closed box for your cat.

10. Decorate the box with colored markers. You could even get creative with different fabrics on the outside of the box.

Glossary

arthritis (ar-THRY-tuhs)—a disease that makes bone joints swollen and painful

circulation (sur-kyuh-LAY-shuhn)—the movement of blood through the body

crepuscular (kri-PUS-kyoo-luhr)—active during twilight

diabetes (dy-uh-BEE-teez)—a disease in which there is too much sugar in the blood

feline distemper (FEE-line diss-TEM-puhr)—a serious and sometimes fatal cat disease that involves fever, vomiting, diarrhea, and dehydration

hairball (HAIR-bawl)—a ball of fur that lodges in a cat's stomach

hydration (hye-DRAY-shuhn)—the act of drinking enough water to stay healthy

prey (PRAY)—an animal hunted by another animal for food

sebum (SEE-buhm)—an oily liquid produced by the skin glands

Read More

Ganeri, Anita. *Kitty's Guide to Caring for Your Cat.* Pets' Guides. Chicago: Capstone Heinemann Library, 2013.

Guillain, Charlotte. *Cats.* Animal Family Albums. Chicago: Capstone Raintree, 2013.

Newman, Aline Alexander, and Gary Weitzman. *How to Speak Cat: A Guide to Decoding Cat Language.* Washington, D.C.: National Geographic, 2015.

Thomas, Isabel. *Cool Cat Projects.* Pet Projects. Chicago: Capstone Raintree, 2016.

🐾 Internet Sites

FactHound offers a safe, fun way to find Internet sites related to this book. All of the sites on FactHound have been researched by our staff.

Here's all you do:

Visit *www.facthound.com*

Type in this code: 9781491483992

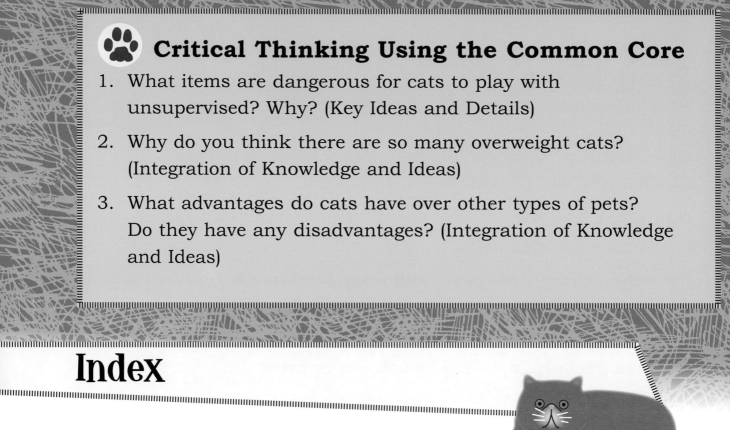

Critical Thinking Using the Common Core

1. What items are dangerous for cats to play with unsupervised? Why? (Key Ideas and Details)

2. Why do you think there are so many overweight cats? (Integration of Knowledge and Ideas)

3. What advantages do cats have over other types of pets? Do they have any disadvantages? (Integration of Knowledge and Ideas)

Index